Musty-Crusty Animals

Hermit Crabs

Lola M. Schaefer

Heinemann Library
Chicago, Illinois

Designed by Sue Emerson/Heinemann Library and Ginkgo Creative, Inc.
Printed and bound in the U.S.A. by Lake Book

06 05 04 03
10 9 8 7 6 5 4 3

Library of Congress Cataloging-in-Publication Data
Schaefer, Lola, M., 1950-
  Hermit crabs / Lola Schaefer.
      p. cm. — (Musty-crusty animals)
Includes index.
Summary: Introduces the physical characteristics, habitat, diet, and
activities of the hermit crab.
  ISBN 1-58810-514-8 (lib. bdg.)   ISBN 1-58810-723-X (pbk. bdg.)
  1. Hermit crabs—Juvenile literature. [1. Hermit crabs. 2. Crabs.] I. Title.
  QL444.M33 S352 2002
  595.3'87—dc21

                               2001003283

Acknowledgments
The author and publishers are grateful to the following for permission to reproduce copyright material:
Title page Doug Perrine; p. 4 Dwight Kuhn; p. 5 Kjell B. Sandved/Visuals Unlimited; p. 6 James Beveridge/Visuals Unlimited; pp. 7, 11 David Liebman; pp. 8, 12, 13, 15R Jeff Rotman Photography; p. 9 Glenn M. Oliver/Visuals Unlimited; pp. 10, 22 Rob & Ann Simpson; p. 14 Eda Rogers; pp. 15L, 18, 19 Jay Ireland & Georgienne E. Bradley/ Bradleyireland.com; p. 16 E. R. Degginger/Color Pic, Inc.; p. 17 Richard Hermann/Seaspics.com; p. 20 C. B. & D. W. Frith; p. 21 Kazunari Kawashima

Cover photograph courtesy of Jeff Rotman Photography

Every effort has been made to contact copyright holders of any material reproduced in this book. Any omissions will be rectified in subsequent printings if notice is given to the publisher.

Special thanks to our advisory panel for their help in the preparation of this book:
Eileen Day, Preschool Teacher
Chicago, IL

Paula Fischer, K–1 Teacher
Indianapolis, IN

Sandra Gilbert,
Library Media Specialist
Houston, TX

Angela Leeper,
Educational Consultant
North Carolina Department
of Public Instruction
Raleigh, NC

Pam McDonald, Reading Teacher
Winter Springs, FL

Melinda Murphy,
Library Media Specialist
Houston, TX

Helen Rosenberg, MLS
Chicago, IL

Anna Marie Varakin,
Reading Instructor
Western Maryland College

Special thanks to Dr. Randy Kochevar of the Monterey Bay Aquarium for his help in the preparation of this book.

Some words are shown in bold, **like this.**
You can find them in the picture glossary on page 23.

Contents

What Are Hermit Crabs?

Hermit crabs are small animals without bones.

They are **invertebrates.**

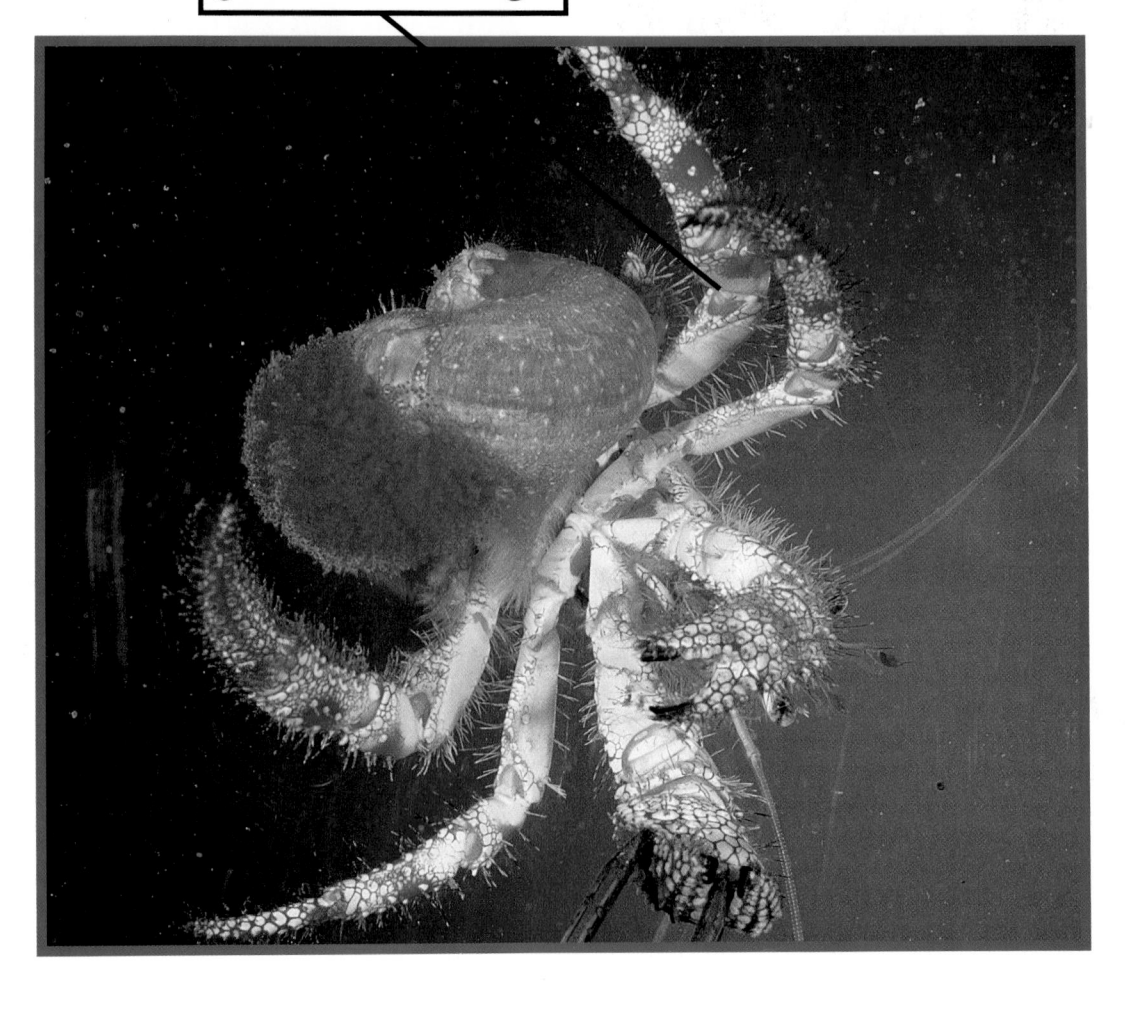

jointed leg

Hermit crabs have **jointed legs.**

Their legs are for walking and holding up a shell.

Where Do Hermit Crabs Live?

Some hermit crabs live on the beach.

Others live in the ocean.

old shell

All hermit crabs live in shells they carry on their backs.

When hermit crabs grow, they move to bigger shells.

What Do Hermit Crabs Look Like?

eyestalks

Hermit crabs look like bugs in shells.

They have two **eyestalks**.

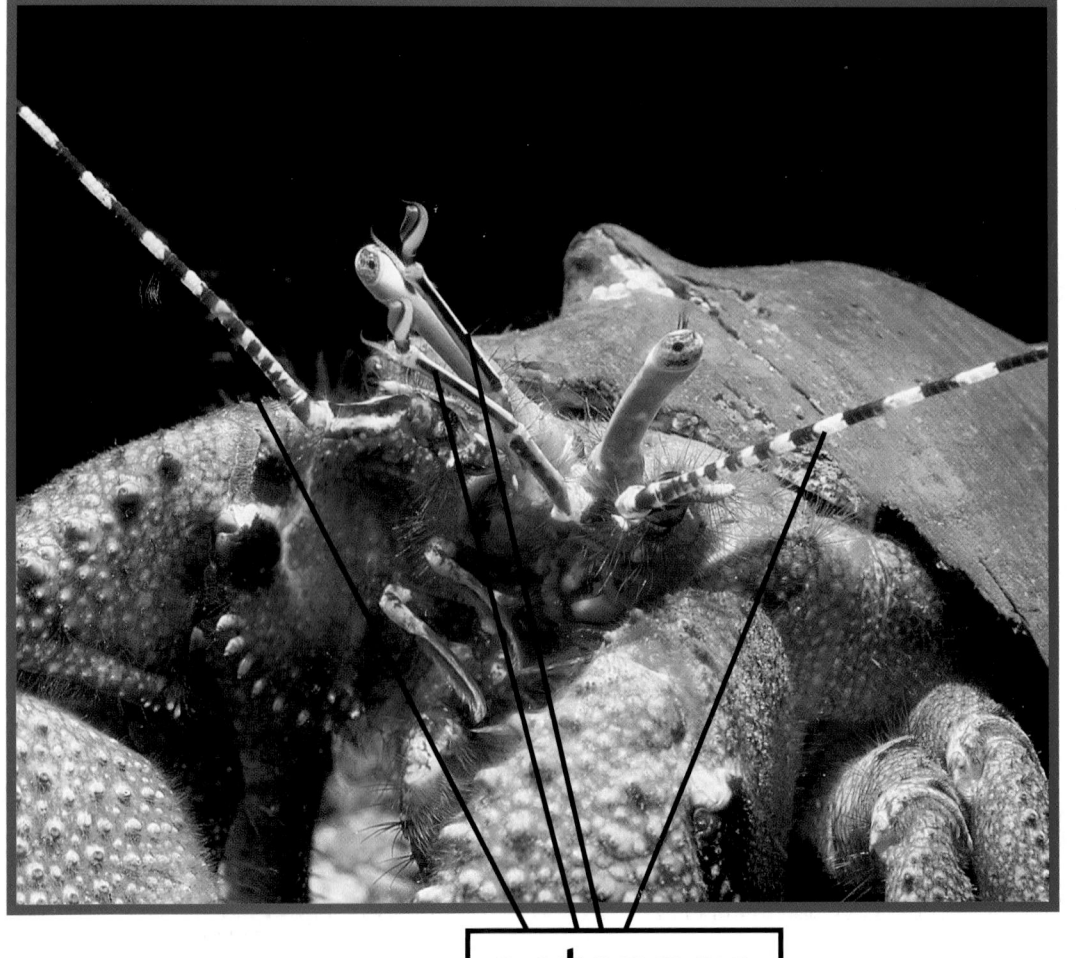

antennae

They have four **antennae.**

These antennae help them feel and smell.

9

Do Hermit Crabs Really Have Shells?

Hermit crabs grow a hard cover on their bodies.

But hermit crabs carry shells on their backs, too.

These are shells other animals have left.

What Do Hermit Crabs Feel Like?

Hermit crabs feel crusty.

The shells they carry feel hard.

claw

Hermit crab **claws** feel stiff and hard.

Their claws are sharp.

How Big Are Hermit Crabs?

Young hermit crabs are smaller than a fingernail.

Adult hermit crabs can be as small as your hand.

Some are as large as tennis balls.

How Do Hermit Crabs Move?

Young hermit crabs swim.

Adult hermit crabs crawl.

Hermit crabs can crawl up, down, and sideways.

They can even crawl over each other.

What Do Hermit Crabs Eat?

seaweed

Hermit crabs eat plants and animals.

They eat the leaves of land plants and **seaweed**.

Hermit crabs eat tiny ocean animals.

They even eat dead animals on the sand.

Where Do New Hermit Crabs Come From?

eggs

Female hermit crabs lay thousands of eggs.

They put the eggs on their bodies.

eggs

Later, they shake the eggs into the ocean.

Young hermit crabs come out of the eggs.

Quiz

What are these hermit crab parts?

Can you find them in the book?

Look for the answers on page 24.

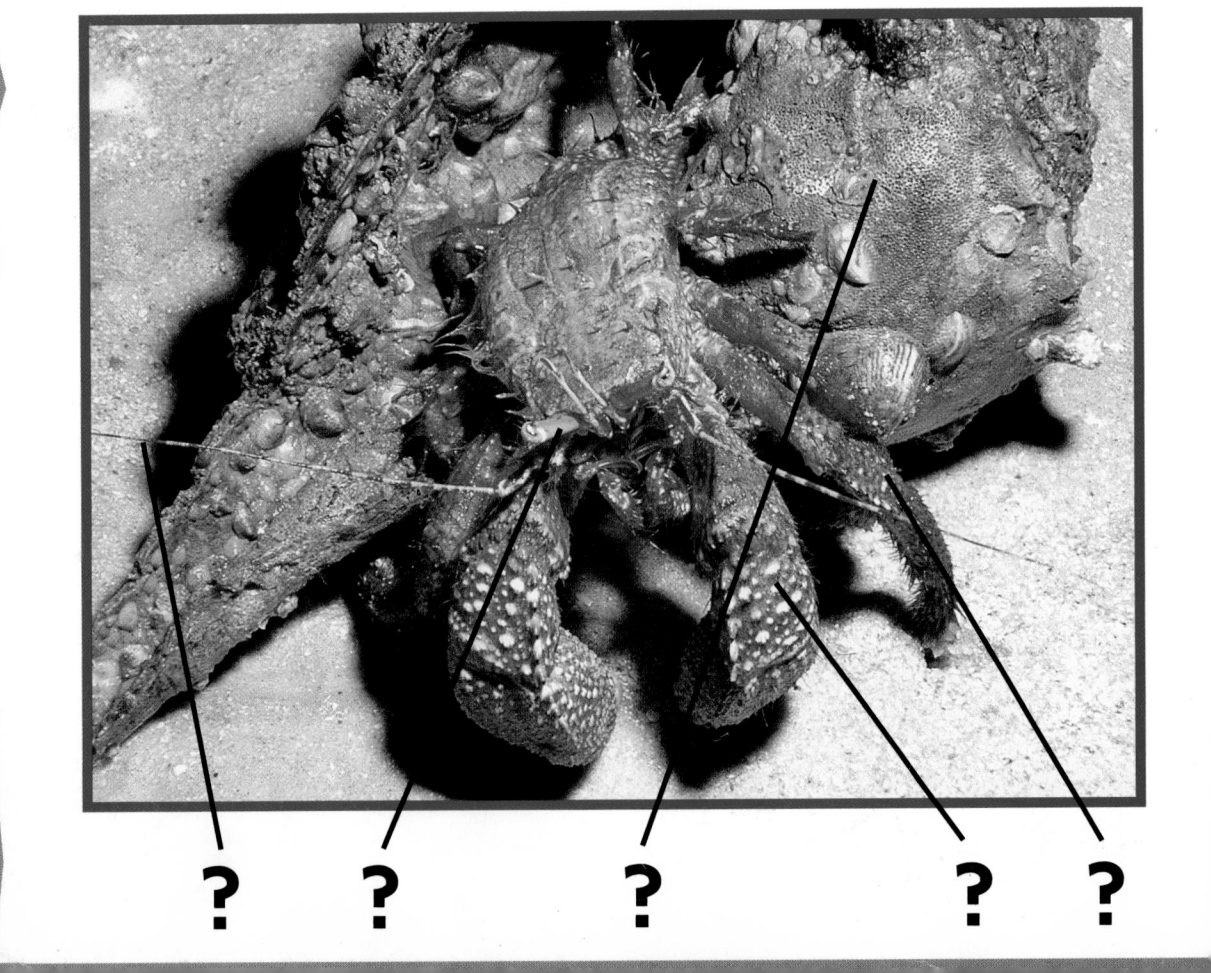

? ? ? ? ?

Picture Glossary

antennae
(an-TEN-ee)
page 9

jointed leg
page 5

claw
page 13

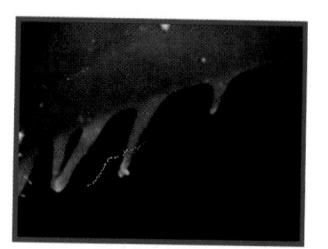
seaweed
page 18

eyestalk
page 8

invertebrate
(in-VUR-tuh-brate)
page 4

Note to Parents and Teachers

Reading for information is an important part of a child's literacy development. Learning begins with a question about something. Help children think of themselves as investigators and researchers by encouraging their questions about the world around them. Each chapter in this book begins with a question. Read the question together. Look at the pictures. Talk about what you think the answer might be. Then read the text to find out if your predictions were correct. Think of other questions you could ask about the topic, and discuss where you might find the answers. Assist children in using the picture glossary and the index to practice new vocabulary and research skills.

! CAUTION: Remind children that it is not a good idea to handle wild animals. Children should wash their hands with soap and water after they touch any animal.

Index

Answers to quiz on page 22

antenna | shell | claw | jointed leg | eyestalk